WHAT PLANT IS THIS?

Everything Science

Marcia S. Freeman

Rourke

Publishing LLC
Vero Beach, Florida 32964

© 2005 Rourke Publishing LLC

PHOTO CREDITS: Cover, pages 9, 11, 16 © Timothy Vacula; title pages, pages 7, 8, 12, 14, 15, 17, 18, 19, 20, 21, 22 © Lynn M. Stone; pages 4, 5, © Lois Nelson; pages 6, 12, 13 © Flanagan Publishing

Library of Congress Cataloging-in-Publication

Freeman, Marcia S.
    What plant is this? (Everything science)

ISBN 1-59515-124-9

Printed in the USA

LK/BK

table of contents

why learn about plants?

Have you ever been the new student in your class? Do you remember how you felt? Were you a little nervous?

When you got to know everyone, it was a lot more fun.

It's nice to have friends at school.

5

Exploring the outdoors

When you know the names of plants, **exploring** the outdoors is a lot more fun too.

Whether you visit a park or a field, knowing the plants makes the visit more exciting.

Careful! Some plants are prickly.

And safer, too. Some plants are **poisonous**!

The state flower of Texas, the bluebonnet, is poisonous to animals. Don't eat it.

When you know some things about a plant, you can look up its name in a **guidebook**.

MISSOURI
FLOWERING DOGWOOD

Scientific Name:
Cornus florida
Year Made State Tree:
1955

When Missouri's spring woodlands are still leafless, the flowering dogwood blooms. Its creamy blossoms brighten woodlands and the slopes along rushing Ozark rivers. In fall, the dogwood's scarlet leaves are like candles among the muted leaves of oaks and hickories.

Dogwoods are slender, spreading trees. They produce clusters of red berries that are food for squirrels, raccoons, and several kinds of songbirds.
(See Virginia, p. 43.)

MONTANA
PONDEROSA PINE

Scientific Name:
Pinus ponderosa
Year Made State Tree:
1949

26

Attributes

You can get to know a plant by noticing things about it. You can notice its **attributes** such as:

- flower color
- flower smell
- petal texture
- leaf size
- leaf shape
- leaf edges
- fruit color
- seed shape
- plant habitat
- ...and more.

How do you think the **petals** of this sego lily feel? Smooth or rough?

Leaves

Are the leaves shaped like a star or an oval? Are the edges smooth or jagged like saw teeth?

This boy is holding a maple leaf.

These leaves (above) are oak leaves.

Do the **veins** in the leaf look like the lines in the palm of your hand or like a feather?

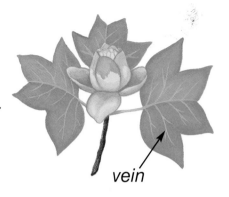

vein

Are the leaves flat and wide or are they more like green needles?

If a tree has long needles, it's a pine.

Flowers

Does the plant have large colorful flowers or small green ones that are hard to see?

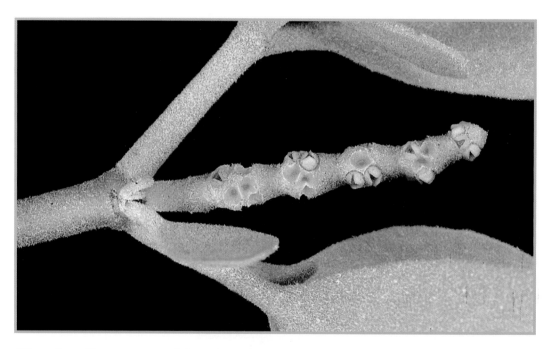

The tiny flowers on this plant have not yet opened.

This sunflower is huge!

How many petals does the flower have? Are the petals separate or do they form a cup?

This flower (above) will turn into a pumpkin!

Fruits and Seeds

The kind of fruit and seeds a plant **produces** will also help you **identify** it.

Do you know the names of these plants?

If a tree has acorns, it's an oak.

If a tree has needles in bunches and produces cones, it's a pine tree.

Habitat

If you know where a plant lives — its habitat — that will help you identify it.

*If a plant grows in the desert and has stems with **spines**, it's a cactus.*

*If a plant grows in a **wetland** and has a brown fuzzy fruit that looks like a cigar, it's a cattail.*

How many plants do you know?

Glossary

attributes (AH truh BYOOTZ) — features of something, such as color and texture

exploring (ek SPLOR ing) — looking at carefully

guidebook (GYD BOOK) — a book of specific information about a place or thing

identify (eye DENT uh FY) — to learn the name of something

petals (PET uhlz) — colorful leaf-like parts of a flower

poisonous (POIZ nus) — able to kill or make sick if eaten

produces (pruh DOOS uz) — makes

spines (SPYNZ) — long, thin plant thorns

veins (VAYNZ) — tubes in plant leaves that carry water

wetland (WET LAND) — land with standing water, a swamp

index

Science Standard: Life Science – Plants
Objects can be described in terms of their physical properties.
Plants and animals have features that help them live in different environments.

Marcia S. Freeman loves writing science books for children. A Cornell University graduate, she has taught science and writing to students from elementary to high school, and their teachers too! Her 50 books also include children's fiction and writing education texts for teachers.